If you love New Kids on the Block you'll want to know everything about them. Together these five handsome guys make great music, but as individuals they're each really different.

1) Who does a great impersonation of Michael Jackson?

2) Who has fond childhood memories of singing in the church choir?

3) Who's more than just friends with Tiffany?

4) Whose favorite food is Mexican?

5) Who wears a gold G-clef earring?

Answers: 1) Donnie 2) Jordan 3) Jon 4) Joe 5) Danny

If you've got New Kids mania, here's the cure!

Be sure not to miss these other exciting
star biographies available from Bantam Starfire
Books

KIRK CAMERON: DREAM GUY
    by Grace Catalano

RIVER PHOENIX: HERO AND HEARTTHROB
    by Grace Catalano

ALYSSA MILANO: SHE'S THE BOSS
    by Grace Catalano

★ ★ ★ ★ ★

NEW KIDS
ON THE
BLOCK

★ ★ ★ ★ ★

by Grace Catalano

BANTAM BOOKS
NEW YORK · TORONTO · LONDON · SYDNEY · AUCKLAND

To Joseph, my brother,
who understands and is always there

NEW KIDS ON THE BLOCK
A Bantam Book / December 1989

The Starfire logo is a registered trademark of Bantam Books, a division of Bantam Doubleday Dell Publishing Group, Inc. Registered in U.S. Patent and Trademark Office and elsewhere.
Bantam edition

ISBN 0-553-28587-4

Bantam Books are published by Bantam Books, a division of Bantam Doubleday Dell Publishing Group, Inc. Its trademark, consisting of the words "Bantam Books" and the portrayal of a rooster, is Registered in U.S. Patent and Trademark Office and in other countries. Marca Registrada. Bantam Books, 666 Fifth Avenue, New York, New York 10103.

PRINTED IN THE UNITED STATES OF AMERICA

20 19

KRI

CONTENTS

NEW KIDS
ON THE
BLOCK

1

POP PHENOMENON

New Kids on the Block. Five young, handsome, talented boys from the Boston, Massachusetts, area. They are, in a word, a sensation.

The band, which includes brothers Jon (age twenty-one) and Jordan Knight (age eighteen), Donnie Wahlberg (age twenty), Danny Wood (age nineteen), and Joe McIntyre (age seventeen), was formed in 1984 by record-producer/songwriter Maurice Starr and Boston manager Mary Alford.

It took the failure of their first album and countless nights playing small clubs to learn their craft and get over the disappointments that come with being in show business. But five years after they came together, they made the big time with a string of top-ten hits.

"The business is sometimes different than what we expected," explains Jon, who is often referred to as the businessman of the group. "There are times when we'll be promised something will happen and then it's canceled. So there's always a lot of disappointment."

Still, the New Kids had the determination and faith in themselves to keep trying, hoping that along the way someone would take notice of them.

It finally happened in 1988.

Their second LP, *Hangin' Tough*, was barely in stores a few months when they got the chance of a lifetime. In the summer of 1988, the group was introduced to Tiffany, teenage pop superstar. Tiffany's manager asked her to listen to the new band and try them as her opening act. It was a case of being in the right place at the right time.

Tiffany was already an established favorite performer among both teenage boys *and* girls. The New Kids stepped into something that seemed as if it couldn't miss—they would not only be Tiffany's opening act, but they would have a teenage audience to sing for.

"When we went out there it was like we

had to prove ourselves," says Donnie. "Tiffany was already an acclaimed act and she didn't really have anything to prove, but we had something to prove going on tour with her—not to her, she was great. She was nice to us from day one. But we had something to prove to America and the Tiffany tour was our chance to do that."

The result was sudden success for the New Kids. It was obvious that what the New Kids had to offer and what the audience wanted matched perfectly. Their polished choreography and harmonic sound, which relies on synthesized funk and rap beats, was an instant hit with teenagers.

Auburn-haired Tiffany describes her teaming with the New Kids by saying, "It worked out great because I have so many girls coming to my shows. And suddenly, there were these five incredibly cute guys up there."

In a matter of months, New Kids on the Block took the music world by storm. As they rapidly rose to stardom, fan mail began to pour into the offices of CBS records.

"Our parents used to run our fan club," says Donnie. "But our record company hired a new company to run our fan club. They told us they received more mail for us than any other act on the label. Michael

Jackson and George Michael record on the same label we do, so that's a lot of mail."

There isn't a teenager today who doesn't know the New Kids or their rockin', rappin' sound. They have taken over as the country's hottest teen heartthrobs, dominating the covers of every major teen magazine both in America and abroad.

The demand for them in Japan is so great, the Kids were flown there for the sole purpose of meeting fans, giving interviews to magazines and the country's MTV, performing on the popular Japanese TV show *Funky Tomato*, and posing for photographs. The guys even filmed a Japanese commercial for a Sony CD player during their brief stay.

New Kids mania is sweeping the country and reaching explosive proportions. Already the statistics surrounding the New Kids phenomenon are staggering. In May 1989, they became the first teen band in history to have three top-ten singles ("Please Don't Go Girl," "I'll Be Loving You (Forever)," and "(You Got It) The Right Stuff" off their *Hangin' Tough* LP)—and that's before their fourth single ("Hangin' Tough") also became a top-ten hit.

Their standing-room-only concerts are always sold out, and their LP *Hangin' Tough* passed the Recording Industry Association of America (RIAA) double-platinum mark. At the third annual Boston Music Awards, the New Kids won for Outstanding Music Video for "(You Got It) The Right Stuff," which, by the way, was also certified RIAA gold.

Over 100,000 phone calls per week flood the New Kids 900 number. Associated Press recently cited the number as one of the most successful 900 numbers. At the same time, 180,000 schoolbook covers (featuring photos of the New Kids) have been distributed to students nationwide via eighty CHR/Gavin stations.

And to meet the demand from their fans, the Kids use their spare time while on tour to appear in record stores, meet the fans face-to-face, and sign autographs. It was reported that stores in Seattle, Portland, Pittsburgh, and Houston were swarming with 5,000 eager teenagers ready to reach out and touch their favorite Kid.

Why are the New Kids so popular with so many teenagers? Maybe part of the reason is because they care about their fans so much. These boys are down-to-earth and levelheaded. They use their spare time wisely by taking part in charity events and want to be sure they are projecting a positive image to their many fans.

As Donnie explains, "When you're in the spotlight, people are going to judge you, so we just try to give them something positive to judge us on."

For one thing, they've been heavily involved with the Just Say No to Drugs campaign since the group was first formed. They joined Massachusetts governor Michael Dukakis's statewide campaign against drugs, doing public service announcements, speaking to groups, and recording a rap song with Boston mayor Raymond L. Flynn. The band's antidrug efforts were recognized when Governor Dukakis named Monday, April 24, 1989, as "New Kids on the Block Day."

They also appeared on the nationally televised United Cerebral Palsy telethon for the third consecutive year. For their work with UCP, they were named teen spokesmen and participated in the organization's annual Bike-A-Thon in New York City in April 1989.

Speaking out on the work they do for countless charities, Jordan says, "It makes us feel great that we're doing something good."

The New Kids, who have been dubbed "The Five Hardest-Working Kids in Show

Business," never want to slow down. Despite their name, these New Kids seem like old pros when it comes to their careers. They know they want to continue striving for bigger things. They've worked too long and they're not about to give anything up just yet.

No doubt the things to come for New Kids on the Block will be even more exciting. While the accomplishments of this hot band are already more than just kid stuff, the group has a lot of plans for the future.

They fancy themselves as the next Beatles. Says Donnie, "We're not happy selling two million albums. We're still in the baby stage. We're only at step one."

2

LIFE BEFORE BECOMING NEW KIDS

The New Kids all hail from the state of Massachusetts. Donnie is from Dorchester, Danny is from Boston, Joe is from Needham, and Jon and Jordan are from Worcester. With the exception of Joe, the kids grew up together, attended school from kindergarten to sixth grade, and hung out on the streets near Boston.

"We're city kids," says Jordan. "They say we're street kids, but we're really not street kids. We're city kids who hung out on the streets."

Jordan's older brother Jon agrees. "We didn't have open fields near us to play ball, so we'd play in the street. In the summer, when we were little, we'd open up the fire hydrant behind our house and have lots of fun."

Donnie Wahlberg, who became known as the band's front man or leader, is very vocal when he speaks about his beginnings living in a tough Boston neighborhood. Born on August 17, 1969, to Alma and Donald, Sr., Donnie grew up in a large family, including three sisters and five brothers. Donnie and his brothers became known as Boston's "legendary tough guys" even though the budding singer occasionally dreamed about another life. First he wanted "to be a baseball star," then he discovered music.

"I guess everyone dreams about being a star," he says. "But I was a very realistic thinker. I didn't sit there and dream about it all day. It didn't occupy my mind because I had too much to worry about living my life every day to start worrying about becoming famous. Where I grew up, that was really farfetched. I never thought the chances were very realistic. What was realistic to me was dealing with problems in my everyday life and life out on the streets."

Still, the thought of entering show business stayed with young Donnie throughout his early years in school. At the age of ten, he and two childhood friends, Billy and

Eric, formed their own band called Risk. "We thought we were really good," he remembers. "But we really weren't. We used to play everything by ear and sometimes it worked out. When that happened, it made us really happy. But it didn't happen often."

At the William Monroe Trotter School in Boston, Donnie met four other kids who, in one way or another, shared some of his dreams and interests in music. One of those kids was Danny Wood.

Like Donnie, Danny was somewhat of a "wild child." "I was a troublemaker" is how he describes himself. Danny, who was born to Daniel and Elizabeth Wood, has three older sisters, one younger brother, and one younger sister.

"My family lives in a big house, but it's not big enough," he says. "I mean, my brother, Brett, and I have always shared a room. I've had a bedroom with him my whole life."

Danny and Donnie became close friends almost instantly. Their common interest in music led them to form their own band.

As Donnie recalls, "Danny, me, and a couple of friends got together and started a band called Kool Aid Bunch. I would write rap routines and we would perform at parties. But it wasn't something that we pursued. It was fun and we loved to do it because we loved having girls screaming for us at parties."

The boys' interest in music prompted them to try out for the school chorus. Danny got in, but Donnie didn't, and their friendship somewhat drifted apart. Danny spent some days after school practicing with the chorus instead of rappin' with Donnie.

It was at practice for the school chorus that Danny met the Knight brothers, Jon and Jordan. They not only sang in school, but also in the church choir. Danny struck up a close friendship with them, especially Jordan. The guys often hung out together, playing basketball and talking about the kind of music they liked.

One summer, Danny and Jordan even decided to get jobs as camp counselors. Today, when Danny thinks about that fun-filled summer, he says, smiling, "That seems so long ago. We were group counselors who taught six- to ten-year-old kids how to dance. We taught them break dancing and took them on trips. It was a lot of fun. I realized how much I really loved kids during that experience."

Jordan Knight and his brother Jon differed from Danny and Donnie. They never found themselves in trouble, nor did they have any interest in hanging around with the tough guys of the neighborhood. Jordan does remember one time when he got into trouble, but it was for something he didn't even do.

"The scariest thing that ever happened to me was when I was real little," he begins. "I was outside this store where kids had just written on the wall on the side of the store. I was just standing there minding my own business when, all of a sudden, the man came out of the store and started chasing me with a gun. He thought I was the one who did the writing. I remember running all the way home without stopping and going straight up to my room. I was so scared."

Jordan and Jon grew up in a unique family environment. Born to Marlene and Allan (now divorced), the brothers had to learn the true meaning of sharing at an early age.

"Our mom would let foster kids stay with us," says Jon. "When we were growing up, we sometimes had ten other brothers and sisters in the house. But I think it was great for us because we learned to get along with all kinds of people."

Biologically, Jon and Jordan have five

brothers and sisters. Their brother Chris was adopted at the age of one right before Jordan was born. "So Chris has been with my family longer than I have," Jordan says, laughing.

Growing up, the Knight brothers were surrounded by music. "My grandparents knew how to read music," begins Jordan. "Plus my dad plays piano, my mom plays the accordion, and my brother David plays bass guitar. He's now the program director at a radio station in college. My nephew Matthew, who is six years old and lives with us, also loves music. He just joined the chorus and is learning the keyboard. When I was little, all my brothers and sisters [including New Kid Jon] sang in the church choir."

At seven years old, Jordan followed in his family's footsteps and joined the church choir, too. It seemed as if this musical beginning was paving the way for a future in music for both Jordan and Jon. However, Jordan sees it differently.

"I can't speak for my brother when I say this," he says, "but even though I was born into a musical family, I never dreamed of being a pop star. I was afraid that guys would be jealous and hate me. I didn't really want to be famous."

On the other side of town, in Needham, Massachusetts, another boy was growing up who *did* have dreams of becoming famous someday. His name was Joseph Mulrey McIntyre.

Joe, who was always ambitious, was born to a tight-knit, talented clan. His parents, Thomas and Kay, always encouraged their children to develop their talents. Joe's thirty-five-year-old sister, Judith, was the first to pursue a career in show business and became a successful New York Broadway stage actress. Joe is very proud of Judith and often likes to talk about her accomplishments. "My sister got rave reviews in the *New York Times* for her portrayal of Peg in the play *Peg of My Heart*," he says. "She's a terrific actress."

Joe's dad even got in on acting when he took time off from his job as vice president of the Boston Bricklayers Union to appear in a commercial for Massachusetts governor Michael Dukakis.

At the age of six, Joe was fully bitten by the performing bug and joined the Neighborhood Children Theatre of Boston. "In my family, whatever one of us does is accepted by the others," he says. "I started acting and singing when I was six right up to when I was twelve and auditioned for the

New Kids. I played the lead role in the musical play *Oliver* with the Children Theatre of Boston. And in one show, my whole family sang the opening song. All except my dad, who sat in the back watching. I really feel that those early years of performing nurtured me for the New Kids."

In 1983, while Joe was content with going to school and appearing onstage in plays on a regular basis, the other four New Kids to be had all gone their separate ways.

Jon and Jordan moved on to a private school while Danny and Donnie temporarily lost touch. "We had all been in school together from kindergarten to about the sixth grade," says Jon. "Then for two years we didn't see each other at all. It was Donnie who brought us all back together again."

3

GETTING STARTED

The concept for New Kids on the Block is
the brainchild of record-producer/song-
writer Maurice Starr, who had formed the
successful black group New Edition, and
Boston manager Mary Alford. As the legend
goes, Starr met Alford, an old friend, on a
Boston street corner one day, and they began talking about forming a streetwise
band that could rap as well as sing and
dance.

New Kids manager Dick Scott says, "Starr
decided to go one step further after New
Edition by creating a group with five young
white boys. White middle America hasn't
had a group like this since the Osmonds."

In the summer of 1984, a citywide search
was conducted for five young guys who

could sing, dance, *and* had unique personalities. It took six months of auditioning countless young hopefuls before Starr decided on a lineup.

Donnie Wahlberg was the first to join the group. He had heard about the auditions through some friends in the neighborhood who told him to try out. Donnie was known in the Boston area for his Michael Jackson impersonations. "I liked being the center of attention and my friends knew that," he says. "They also knew that I rapped and danced a little and thought I'd be ready, willing, and able to give something like this a shot."

What his friends didn't know was that Donnie originally had second thoughts before deciding to audition. "I had seen Maurice's record in the store," he says. "And I saw New Edition's record with his name on it. I thought, 'This dude is going to want a singer, and if I'm not a good singer, I'm not going to make it.'" So Donnie made up his mind to just forget the whole thing.

But somehow he couldn't forget it. His friends kept pushing him to go for it, and deep down inside, he really *did* want to go in and see what it was all about. He told himself that he didn't care what the outcome would be; he simply wanted to satisfy himself and try out. With that outlook, he left for the audition, taking his younger brother, Mark, with him.

Starr immediately saw something special in the fifteen-year-old and signed up a surprised Donnie on the spot. Having been in the business for so many years, Starr had a keen eye for spotting future talent. He'd done it before with New Edition and Bobby Brown, the singer who started out with the group and later went on to achieve success as a solo artist.

"Maurice felt I had good qualities, leadership qualities and potential to be onstage in front of a lot of people," confides Donnie. "He showed me that I could become a good singer, even though I didn't think I could. I rapped and danced, and Maurice welcomed me aboard and told me he'd help me out and develop my talents. He gave me the confidence I really needed."

Starr also liked the idea of having two brothers in the band and signed Donnie's brother Mark to the group as well. However, Mark chose to drop out early on.

"Mark and me *were* the group for about three months, but he was having trouble wanting to become a singer," says Donnie. "He was having too much fun with his life the way it was. He wanted to play basketball.

He wasn't happy being in the group, so he didn't do it and he did what made him happy. I really respect him for that."

With Donnie the only member of the still-unnamed band, Starr asked him if he knew any other guys with musical talent. Without hesitation, Donnie immediately thought of Danny Wood and the Knight brothers. "They were the first and only guys I could find that I knew could do it," he says.

It took a lot of persuading on Donnie's part, but he finally convinced Danny, Jordan, and Jon to try out for the group. All three were chosen even though Jordan wasn't completely comfortable with the idea.

"When I joined the New Kids, I wasn't sure if it was the right thing to do," he says. "It was after about a year of being in the group that I really knew I wanted to be part of it."

With four members selected, Donnie asked another friend, Jamie, to audition. He was also chosen, but as with Mark, it didn't work out. After six weeks, he dropped out of the band.

"He was a really good friend of mine," says Donnie. "I think he might regret leaving the group. But he wasn't into it at all and his family didn't want him involved in show business."

Before deciding on the fifth and final member, Starr went back to his original idea. He had wanted one band member to be younger than the rest like Donny Osmond had been to the Osmonds and Michael Jackson had been to the Jackson 5 in the 1970s. Someone who could complement the other guys, by being the one who would appeal to preteens, while the rest would appeal to teens.

Starr met Joe McIntyre on Father's Day, June 15, 1985, and was so impressed by his enthusiasm and talent that he signed him that very same day. "Mary [Alford] picked me up and I was really scared," remembers Joe about his audition. "I went to Maurice's house and tried out. I sang one of the songs the group was about to record, and afterwards we got in the car and Mary asked me, 'Well, do you want to be in the group? You've got the part.' And I said, 'Yeah, here I am,' and we recorded the songs."

The hardest part for Joe was being accepted by the rest of the guys. "At first, it was weird because Joe was twelve years old," says Jon. "We used to pick on him and give him a hard time. But now he's like our little brother."

"We didn't accept him at first because our good friend was leaving," says Donnie. "We didn't know Joe because he was from a different neighborhood. He looked kind of square and we weren't sure if he was going to fit in, but he proved to us that he fits in good."

The more Donnie got to know Joe, the more he felt like an older brother watching out for him. "I used to bully him a lot, but I really tried to keep him in line and keep his head straight," offers Donnie. "My brothers did that for me and now I appreciate it, so I wanted to do it for Joe. I realized what a great guy he is. I look at him and I see a younger version of me. Joe's a lot like me."

The group was finally complete, and now that Starr had five talented guys ready to rock, he began working on a sound, an image, and most important, a name.

For their name, he came up with Nynuk, a moniker that prompted too much teasing from the guys' friends. They'd ask them things like, "Which one of you guys is Nynuk of the North?" The name also posed a problem for the band during early interviews with magazines. For one thing, they thought it was embarrassing; for another, it didn't seem like a good name for an up-and-coming rock band.

They wanted to change it, but it took a while to decide on a new name. It was after they recorded one of their first rap tunes called "New Kids on the Block" that they found what they were looking for. The name seemed perfect, and the five-member band became known as New Kids on the Block from that day forward.

Their image was to be clean-cut, all-American, and at the same time, hip. In the beginning, the fivesome didn't get involved with the band's songs, even though Donnie and Danny had been writing songs since their days as part of the band Kool Aid Bunch. Instead, they chose to leave the songwriting and planning to Maurice Starr.

By September 1985, a four-song demo tape was completed and shipped to major record labels. While Starr waited for responses, he didn't keep his band idle. He booked them to play concerts where they'd gain some stage experience.

The five guys credit Starr completely for making the band the success it is today. He taught them everything he knew, passing on invaluable tips. He showed them dance steps and worked around the clock with them on style and sound. Under Maurice

Starr's watchful eye, the New Kids rehearsed regularly, after school and on weekends. When it got too difficult for them, Starr was there to encourage them. He could see they liked it, even though sometimes it seemed like more work than they thought it would be.

When that happened, Starr helped them even more. He wanted to prove to them that all the work they were doing was going to be worth it.

The first time the New Kids performed in public was at a prison on Deer Island, Massachusetts. Though the experience was somewhat unnerving, the New Kids put on a great show. "They loved us!" says Donnie enthusiastically.

Jon remembers that first show even more vividly because he had to overcome the feeling of "severe stage fright." Although all the kids, including Jon, are prone to occasional "butterflies" before a concert, Jon says, "I didn't eat for a week before that first show. And when I got onstage, my knees shook. I was *very* nervous."

Maurice Starr was extremely pleased with the reaction the New Kids received from their first show and began booking the Kids for a string of concert appearances in and around Boston. Appearing in concerts in primarily black neighborhoods, the New Kids gained an audience.

"It's easy for us to relate to our success with black fans," says Danny. "When we started out, we did most of our shows in black neighborhoods. Our producers felt that if we could perform in front of black audiences and get over, we could go anywhere and get over."

It worked. The New Kids became stronger at performing because, as Danny says, "We had to be so much better than if we played for white kids. We knew they'd accept us easier."

This way, the New Kids would have a much larger following of fans plus they could become a crossover band on the charts. In other words, their music could become hits on the R&B, rap, pop, rock, and dance charts—if they were signed to a record label.

By Christmas 1985, they still hadn't heard anything positive from the labels Maurice Starr had sent their demo to. Still, the guys felt they'd hear something positive soon. After all, Donnie says, it was destiny that brought the New Kids together, and it was going to be destiny that would take them to the top.

They waited and wondered what would

happen, unaware of the fact that success would soon be knocking on their door. In less than one month, the lives of Donnie Wahlberg, Danny Wood, Joe McIntyre, Jon Knight, and Jordan Knight would never be the same again.

4

COUNTDOWN TO STARDOM

In January 1986, New Kids on the Block landed a contract with Columbia Records. The label signed the band to the company's black-music division and planned to release their debut album later in the year.

It was the chance the kids and producer Maurice Starr had been hoping for. The New Kids were ready. All they needed now was a hit record. Up until that time, the band's future seemed uncertain. They were at a virtual standstill, performing sporadic shows, first one night a week, then one night a month.

Donnie remembers when the band was just starting out. They'd be dreaming about becoming celebrities, while, at the same time, they'd go on with their lives as if nothing were altering them.

"Being in the band was all so new to us back when we were first starting out," says Donnie. "I look back at the times when we first began singing together and how much fun we had even though we were only performing one night every few weeks.

"We'd be like heroes for that one night onstage, and then the next day, we would wake up, get in the subway, and go to school. All of a sudden, we were back to being normal kids."

Donnie feels that because the band kept trying to climb up the ladder of success, they were, in the end, rewarded greatly for their efforts. "To be in show business, you have to take the initiative and go for things," he says. "And that's how we are, how we've always been."

In early April 1986, "Be My Girl," the band's very first single, was released. It immediately generated positive responses from dance deejays. New Kids on the Block made a good first impression on music fans and music-industry executives.

Maurice Starr and the record company wanted to build them up as a hot, new teen band, complete with sequined stage outfits and bubblegum, teenybop music. They saw these five young, good-looking singers as pinup boys in teen and rock magazines. The band, undoubtedly, had the talent and the right moves. And the record executives were going to give them what they felt the right "look" should be.

After the release of "Be My Girl," the New Kids quickly began recording what was to become their debut album. All seemed to be running smoothly and on schedule. The New Kids were being hyped as the next big teen sensation of the day. The only problem was none of the guys liked their new image.

"They wanted us to be this little preppy teen kind of band," says Jon. Danny explains, "We went with the flow and didn't say much about what *we* wanted to do. We had other ideas for the band, but we wouldn't say anything. We had just gotten into the business and didn't know a lot about the way things were run."

The guys went along with the original image planned for them, unhappy with it but never letting anyone know. Their first LP would be released in the summer of 1986. But before it hit record stores, the New Kids made some appearances in New York and in their hometown to introduce some tracks off their self-titled album.

First, they joined the July 4th Statue of Liberty festivities in New York, performing their rap tune "New Kids on the Block" for thousands of enthusiastic fans. They appeared as part of the "City Kids Speak Out on Liberty" program at Battery Park. Gaining much-needed exposure, they also opened for the Four Tops at the Kite Festival back home in Dorchester and for Lisa Lisa and Cult Jam at an "over twenty-one" club—9 Lansdowne—in Boston.

Though they had two more hit singles— "Stop It Girl" and a remake of the Delfonics 1970 Philly soul classic "Didn't I (Blow Your Mind)"—their first album didn't skyrocket the band to the top, as they had hoped.

In fact, the rest of 1986 and most of 1987 were low points for the New Kids. What had gone wrong was still unclear. All they knew was that they had gained enough attention to get a second chance. The New Kids and Maurice Starr weren't about to stop now.

What they needed desperately was something big to help them get their names up in lights. They needed to reach an audience with a new look, a new image, and a new sound.

5

HANGIN' TOUGH

Hangin' Tough put the New Kids on the rock and roll map. The guys all admit that they weren't really prepared for the overwhelming positive response their second album received.

"I think we always knew we'd be successful someday," offers Donnie. "But when it came, it was a big surprise."

As soon as the promotion was completed for their first album, the New Kids packed away their sequined suits and got right to work on what was to become *Hangin' Tough*. This time, the boys decided to talk to Maurice Starr about what they wanted the band to be. They planned for the second album to go in a completely different direction. One thing they took into account while working on the new album was the growth the band had gone through since their inception.

At this time, Danny didn't think the band would be successful. "After our first album didn't do very well, I didn't know what to think," he says. "I decided that I wanted to be a good singer and we all got together and really worked on our second album, *Hangin' Tough*. We all set out to create the best album we could."

Maurice Starr wrote, produced, and arranged an LP that mixed together a sophisticated blend of rap, funk, soul, and rock. Boasting the best of the New Kids material to date, the finished product had everyone excited. The LP also marked the first time Danny, Donnie, and Jordan had worked as a songwriting team.

As associate producers and cowriters (with Starr) on "My Favorite Girl," the trio discovered an entirely new end of the recording business. Danny, especially, is interested in learning more about engineering. They dubbed themselves The Crickets, which derives from the street lingo where a gang is called a posse or a crew, and plan to continue working behind the scenes on all future New Kids albums.

Danny explains, laughing, "We're not a

crew or anything. We're like nice guys, so it was funny. There's one posse called the Jamaican Dog Posse, so we were saying, 'Let's be the Mice Posse.' We just came up with The Crickets' cause Crickets make music, too."

A memorable moment for the New Kids had been making their national TV debut on *Star Search.* But an even more important time was the release of *Hangin' Tough.* It seemed as if the band had started all over again. Their high energy was still there; in concert, so were their exciting dance routines. What they chose to eliminate were the sequined outfits and the bubblegum music.

"We wanted to be more ourselves," says Jon. "We wanted to come out a little more street. We grew up a great deal in the time between the first album and *Hangin' Tough.* So we felt we had to have a more grown-up image. The first album was bubblegum, and I guess everyone does associate bubblegum with cutesy little kids."

Jordan is quick to point out, "*Hangin' Tough* is the kind of album that goes out to everybody. Pop, dance, and R&B."

Donnie explains, "*Hangin' Tough,* in our eyes, is the symbol of us. Our first album was sort of what people wanted us to be, maybe a mold or something. These are the New Kids on the Block, they're nice, good-looking, young guys, they sing nice bubble-gum music. But that's not really what we feel we are. We just feel we're us, we're individuals, and we wanted to be portrayed more as us than we were on the first album."

The guys were careful about the tough, streetwise image they were giving the band. They wanted to be sure that kids realized they were both streetwise and *good.* "A lot of people associate musicians with drugs, craziness, and bad people," says Jon. "But that's not what we want this group to be."

New Kids on the Block would still be five clean-cut teenagers, but with more of an edge, some roughness. "Most of us are from the streets, except Joe, but we're not hoods or anything," notes Danny. "It's kind of a street image that kids can relate to. Before we got into the group, I was into the streets—not the drug scene or anything. I was into the break-dancing scene, but I was on the streets a lot. Joining the group was something like playing basketball. If you play basketball, you can stay off the street, you can set a goal for yourself. Music has made a goal for us."

Though it's true that the New Kids were

raised in the city and admit to hanging out on the streets, it's also true that these boys were serious about working and going to school.

Most of the guys had after-school and summer jobs. Donnie and his father drove a truck and delivered food to schools and summer camps.

Danny's ambition was to become an architect. He was an A student and had a four-year scholarship to Boston University. But he had his mind on the group and learning about recording. "I couldn't really concentrate on school because I wanted to do this so bad," he says. "I was into going to the studio every day, because I was learning about engineering. So I left school. But I still have my scholarship and I know I can go back anytime I want in the future. I feel so lucky to have been chosen for the New Kids, and right now, I want to give my all to the band."

Danny admits that his parents were totally against his decision to leave school. Though they became supportive of him later, they were skeptical in the beginning.

"My father told me, 'If you leave school, you have to get a real job,' " says Danny. "So I was a courier delivering airline tickets for about six months. Then *Hangin' Tough* took off, and after we had our first hit with 'Please Don't Go Girl,' I quit."

Donnie always found it easy to juggle his schoolwork with his songwriting. "I began writing rap songs while I was in school and it never interfered with school—unless I let it!" he says.

After the New Kids caught on with audiences, they began a tour that would take them away from their lives as regular high school students. They had been studying with a tutor on and off since the release of their first album, but now a full-time tutor was assigned to the guys. "When the group started to pick up, I started to take school a little more seriously," says Donnie.

It was Joe, the youngest member of the band, who found the adjustment hard at first. "It's kind of tough missing out on going to a regular high school," he says with sadness in his voice. "The other guys already had most of their high school years, but I was just getting into high school. Before we started touring, I was almost the perfect student. I did all my homework, studied for every test. I had a blast in school. Then, all of a sudden, it changed."

Both Jon and Jordan saw the band as "a once-in-a-lifetime opportunity." Though the Knight brothers would like to attend college eventually, they feel being New Kids is giving them the best learning experience they could ever have.

By the early summer of 1988, the release of "Please Don't Go Girl" put the Kids on top, and two more singles—"I'll Be Loving You (Forever)" and "(You Got It) The Right Stuff"—were quickly being rushed out. Yet it was only after they started to tour with Tiffany as her opening act that the world began to take note of this five-member band.

An interesting thing happened right before the guys met Tiffany, which they will never forget. A friend of Donnie's went to a palm reader and asked what the future held for the band. She responded that a young girl would help them become famous. The following week they met Tiffany and went on tour with her. "It was very weird," Jon says. "We still can't believe it!"

Tiffany remembers her now-famous meeting with the New Kids very clearly. "I was on tour and my agent told me about a new group called New Kids on the Block," she begins. "He said, 'They're here and they want to come in and perform for you.' I thought, Now? I had just gotten something to eat. But then I remembered when I was twelve and I would audition for someone who was eating and they'd say, 'That was really good,' even if they weren't paying any attention.

"So I just set my food aside and they came in. It was a small room and they started to dance. Because the room was so small, they were hitting each other in the face. My girlfriend Sue was there, and they were introduced to us one by one.

"Then Jerry, my agent, and George, my manager, said, 'Why don't we put them in the show tonight and just take a chance? They've got a tape and they sing live to prerecorded tapes.' I said, 'Sure,' and they went into the show," concludes Tiffany.

That first meeting took place in Tiffany's dressing room at the Westbury Music Fair, a popular theater in the round on Long Island, New York, and that night the New Kids burst onto that round stage and made music history. Most of the time, an opening act for an established performer doesn't go over favorably with audiences. The New Kids, however, were greeted with an enthusiastic response as Tiffany's opening act. The teaming of Tiffany and the New Kids was double dynamite right from that first show they did together. And that one shot proved New Kids on the Block were one hot, rising band to keep an eye on.

"I consider the tour with Tiffany our breaking into the business," says Jordan. "It was breaking the ice with the people in her organization, the road crew, and just getting to know them. After we did that, everything went fine."

Word spread quickly about New Kids on the Block. The five adorable guys began winning the hearts of millions of fans. Anyone who doubted their talents earlier was now applauding them.

New Kids mania was beginning to take shape.

6

THE FAB FIVE ONSTAGE

The concert wasn't scheduled to begin for another hour, but excited New Kids fans were already arriving. In the lobby, hundreds of teenagers and preteens, most of them girls, were talking and laughing. The excitement in their voices almost drowned out the shouts of the men selling New Kids on the Block souvenir tourbooks, T-shirts, and posters.

The screaming began long before the New Kids appeared onstage. This was the concert all their fans had been looking forward to for weeks, and they couldn't hide their emotions. These fans didn't just come to hear the New Kids sing. They could do that in their own bedrooms by listening to their records. They came to be with the New Kids, to see them in person and maybe even to meet one of them close up.

As the anticipation mounted out front, backstage there was just as much going on as Donnie, Danny, Joe, Jon, and Jordan began getting ready to give yet another electrifying concert. Over the last few months, they had not only opened for Tiffany but headlined many of their own shows as well.

One thing they all do before each show is drink a special blend of honey and lemon tea. "Our music director, Greg McPherson, told us that drinking tea with lemon and honey would soothe our throats so we could sing better," says Jordan.

But besides drinking tea and using tons of hairspray to keep their hair in place, the New Kids have a long list of things they like to do before every concert. Donnie, for one, has a personal lucky superstition that's worked for him throughout the band's last few headlining shows. Inspired by the success of recent stars Don Johnson and George Michael, Donnie never shaves before going onstage.

Probably the most important preconcert ritual is the one they've done before every show since the band's very first concert. "We all get in a huddle and yell a lot and tell each other to go out there and give the best concert possible," says Donnie. "Then we start throwing fake punches and shaking each other up to get ourselves going. And then, right before we go onstage, just as they announce our name, we run past our manager and slap his hand!"

From behind the curtain, the New Kids could hear the fans yelling in unison, "We want the New Kids!" "We want the New Kids!" as they get ready to go on. But before they do, the lights dim for a few seconds, the drum begins a slow, steady beat, and the beginning of their song "My Favorite Girl" is playing. Then with dazzling swiftness, as the spotlights light up the stage, New Kids on the Block leap from the midst of this frenzy—dancing, prancing, and stepping high. They come out singing, but for several moments, the screams are so loud, it is difficult to hear them.

A New Kids concert is a happening. Once onstage, the fab five launch into song, singing in clear voices and reaching out to touch the hands of lucky fans in the front. The crowd falls silent, but not for long. The slightest quiver in the voices of the five talented guys onstage brings a chorus of shrieks and screams from the audience.

For anyone who has attended a New Kids

concert, all seems perfect. Their concerts are top-notch from their carefully staged dance routines to the sound equipment and the superb lighting. There have been times, though, when certain incidents, surprising and embarrassing, caught these skilled performers off guard.

During one of their early concerts with Tiffany, they went out to play one night and weren't given cordless microphones. "The cords were everywhere," recollects Danny. "When Jordan began to sing his lead part on 'The Right Stuff,' I stepped right on my mike cord, which made it real tight—and my mike went flying out into the audience."

Other concerts that stand out in their minds occurred at Six Flags Magic Mountain amusement park, just outside Los Angeles, California. Originally booked for two shows, the band agreed to do a third because the demand was so great.

At a New Kids concert, it is no surprise to see gifts being tossed onto the stage as the guys perform. In fact, at the end of a concert, the stage is usually filled with everything from hats to teddy bears to balloons to bouquets of flowers.

During their second concert at Magic Mountain, the audience began tossing pennies, nickels, dimes, and quarters onto the stage. At first, the guys overlooked it, but when the coins nearly hit Jon's head, he asked the crowd to stop throwing them or the band would have to end the show. When the fans didn't stop, the guys did cut the concert short. They never came up with any clues as to why the audience was throwing the coins. And it remains one of their strangest onstage experiences to date.

Another moment they will never forget also happened during one of their concerts at Magic Mountain. Donnie is the guy who is always winking and waving at the girls in the audience. As he was performing "Hangin' Tough," he took center stage and directed his attention to a girl sitting in a wheelchair in the front. As he moved closer to the edge of the stage to reach down and extend his hand to the girl, she stood up and tried to jump onstage. It turned out she just used the wheelchair to get closer to her favorite New Kid.

Of course, while there are many stories to tell about the audiences during these concerts, there are just as many stories to tell *about* the New Kids. In a concert in Florida recently, Donnie fell off the stage and didn't realize at first that he'd split his finger and knee open and ripped his clothes.

In another concert in Florida, Jordan had

an embarrassing, but fun, experience when he fell into the crowd of adoring fans. "There was a space between the stage and the audience where it was security guards," begins Jordan, flashing his gorgeous smile. "It was like an open space and I jumped in and I tripped on something and fell near the crowd. The girls grabbed me. Some grabbed my hair. They ripped my jacket off. All the girls started to fight over it and they started ripping it up. I think everyone in the front row had a piece of my jacket. It was great for me, but I think it was scary for the bodyguards," concludes Jordan, laughing.

During that first summer in 1988, the New Kids spent six weeks touring with Tiffany. Following their initial success, they embarked on a one-month headlining tour before reuniting with Tiffany for a second leg of her tour. It was during their second time touring with Tiffany that the Kids decided to get a complete band of musicians to play backup instead of continuing to use prerecorded music. And they decided it was time *they* played instruments onstage as well.

The guys didn't play on their two previous albums because they were each diligently studying an instrument. Now they thought the time was right to give their fans an extraspecial treat during their concerts.

"During our recent shows, we changed a few things," says Jordan. "Each one of us has a turn at taking the stage and talking to the audience. Plus now we play instruments. Some people don't think we can play, but we do it just to show them we can. We call it the New Kids Groove. We all jump up with our instruments and play. It's like a big jam session."

One thing that is certain is that the New Kids *love* performing onstage. In concerts, it always makes them happy to have one-on-one contact with their fans. Though most of these fans are girls, boys also love the New Kids' chart-topping music. "It's nice when guys are supportive, too," explains Donnie. "A lot of times with young guy groups, other guys tend to be jealous and don't give them a chance, but a lot of guys support us and that's important to us. It's real inspiring to look out in the crowd and see a guy waving his fist or cheering or singing along with us. It means that people are judging us for our music and our abilities."

Of all the concerts the New Kids have performed, the highlight of their career was playing at the Apollo Theater in New York

City. It was a dream come true for the guys because they had always heard so much about the theater and the bands who played it. As Jordan exclaims, "The greatest thing for all of us was when we played at the Apollo. We got a standing ovation, and then they brought us back for a second night and everything. It was touching. It was like being a millionaire and stumbling on top of a million dollars."

What is it that makes this band so special? Perhaps Donnie says it best. "I think we're not clones of each other," he reveals. "We are five guys who are ourselves. When I'm onstage, I get real intense and real serious, and that's me. I appeal to some of the crowd, and maybe Jordan appeals to some of the crowd, and Danny's style, and Jon's shining—we all have a different appeal, and we bring out our own personalities in everything we do. A lot of the other groups all have the same suit on and don't really show any personality. I respect other groups, but I think that's the difference with our group."

Nothing had prepared the New Kids for the many changes that sudden fame would bring to their lives in one single year.

7

THE SCOOP ON THE GUYS—
AND THEIR RAP
ABOUT GIRLS

The New Kids seem to have time for everything these days—recording, writing songs, touring. The only thing they can't seem to squeeze into their busy schedules is girls and dating. Because they are constantly on the go, they find it difficult to maintain relationships. However, that doesn't stop the guys from explaining the kind of girls they like, or talking about their idea of a perfect date.

Before the New Kids rap about the kind of girls they like, it's a good idea to get to know a little more about the five guys. What are they *really* like?

★

MEET DONNIE WAHLBERG

By now it must seem obvious to New Kids fans that this blondish-brown-haired guy is the group's spokesman. Whenever a reporter asks to interview the New Kids, whether it be over the phone or in a hotel lounge, it is Donnie who will answer the majority of the questions. Donnie is the kind of guy who likes to put other people at ease. Donnie's favorite singer is Bobby Brown, and when Donnie is interviewed he sometimes breaks into rappin' rhymes.

Energetic, soft-spoken, and outgoing, Donnie surprisingly describes himself as "lazy because when I'm finished putting my energy in, I like to just sleep all day." When he is done with a full day's work or has some rare time off, Donnie enjoys a brisk game of baseball or basketball. His favorite hobbies include dancing and, in quieter moments, drawing.

Donnie admits he loves "girls of all races, shapes, and sizes." He hasn't had time to date that much, but he can't forget his first love.

"My first love was a great learning experience," he explains. "It taught me a lot. I was

NEW KIDS ON THE BLOCK

New Kids on the Block are (l to r) Donnie
Wahlberg, Danny Wood, Jordan Knight,
Joe McIntyre, and Jon Knight.

(Photo by Nick Elgar/London Features)

A New Kids concert is always exciting. These five kids from Boston (l to r) Donnie, Jon, Danny, Joe, and Jordan keep their fans dancing in the aisles.

(Photo by Janet Macoska)

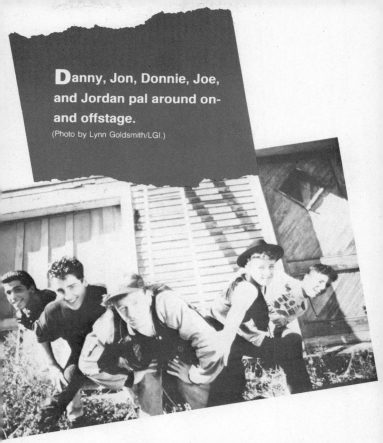

Danny, Jon, Donnie, Joe, and Jordan pal around on- and offstage.

(Photo by Lynn Goldsmith/LGI.)

NEW KIDS
ON THE
BLOCK

Handsome Jon is
the oldest "kid."

(Photo by Michele Hoffman)

NEW KIDS ON THE BLOCK

Five fantastic guys.
(Photo by Vinnie Zufante/Star File)

Adorable Joe sings ''Please Don't Go Girl'' to lucky fans in the first row.

(Photo by Janet Macoska)

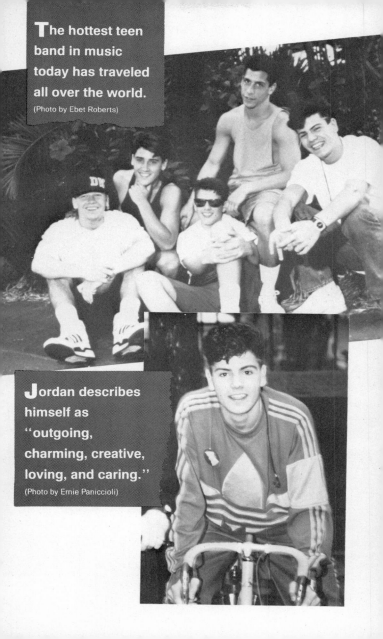

The hottest teen
band in music
today has traveled
all over the world.
(Photo by Ebet Roberts)

Jordan describes
himself as
"outgoing,
charming, creative,
loving, and caring."
(Photo by Ernie Paniccioli)

With lights flashing and fans cheering, Donnie sings the New Kids' hot hit song, "Hangin' Tough."

(Photo by Janet Macoska)

The New Kids love you, their loyal fans.

(Photo by Ernie Paniccioli)

Brothers Jon and Jordan rock onstage and drive the crowd wild.

(Photo by Janet Macoska)

NEW KIDS
ON THE
BLOCK

The New Kids perform on
the Kids Choice Award show
on the Nickelodeon cable
channel.

(Photo by Vinnie Zuffante/Star File)

Danny takes a break during a rehearsal at Westbury Music Fair.

(Photo by Ernie Paniccioli)

As the teen spokesmen for United Cerebral Palsy, the New Kids participated in the United Cerebral Palsy Bike-a-Thon in New York City.

(Photo by Ernie Paniccioli)

A portrait of New Kids on the Block. Each band member has his very own style.

(Photo by Lynn Goldsmith/LGI.)

NEW KIDS
ON THE
BLOCK

"**T**his is just the beginning," says Donnie of the band's future. "We want to go back out and do more. Whatever we did before we want to double."

(Photo by Lynn Goldsmith/LGI.)

NEW KIDS ON THE BLOCK

very much in love, and the girl I was in love with left me for another guy."

Donnie's first girlfriend went back to her old boyfriend, who had moved back to the town they lived in. Though it broke Donnie's heart at the time, he says, "I still hear from her. She's still a nice girl."

What kind of girl does Donnie like? "I like a strong, independent girl who won't rely on my personality," he says. "Sometimes you can see a guy and a girl together and you can see a dominant personality. A guy gets strength from the girl, and the girl gets strength from the guy. I like a girl who can find strength in herself, and is not going to like me because I'm in a group. She'll like me for who I am."

Donnie's favorite way to spend an evening with a girl is to go to a nice restaurant for a quiet dinner, followed by a movie or a walk around Boston. In the summer months, he likes to go to amusement parks, but he makes it clear to the girl he's with that he doesn't like going on Ferris wheels.

"I won't ever go on another one," he confesses. "I just think they are the most dangerous ride in an amusement park. They're so easy to fall out of. I was on one of them once with a friend and we stopped at the top. My friend was shaking the car back and forth. It was terrifying. I tell you what I love, though, are roller coasters. I ride them all, stand-up, triple-loop. They're great!"

Donnie describes himself as "very generous, very serious. I love talking and I'm always thinking. I love to be in love." Donnie has clear goals of success in the music industry, but he definitely wants to have fun doing it. He loves to eat and is glad that even though he can eat all day he stays skinny.

MEET DANNY WOOD

Danny has been described by the other guys as "sensitive," "stubborn," "real funny," and a "great kid." It is a little-known fact that black-haired Danny is deeply attached to a teddy bear that was given to him when he was born.

"I've had it with me all my life," he says. "They don't make them anymore, so I guess you can call it an antique."

Coming from a family of six brothers and sisters, Danny is very closely connected to his family. He claims that his most treasured memory from childhood is when his younger sister Rachel was born, and one thing he really values is the time he gets to spend with his mom.

Of course, being part of New Kids on the Block doesn't leave Danny much free time, but when he does have some time off from touring and recording, he enjoys writing songs and playing basketball.

Danny is proud of the choreographing he does for the group. He and Jon especially combine steps and energy for the group's routines.

On the subject of dating, Danny says his ideal girl is "someone who I can talk to and who is fun, nice, honest, and easygoing."

Though he admits to getting scared when he goes to see horror movies, it's his number-one choice for a date. "The worst horror movie I ever saw was *The Shining*," admits Danny. "But I love horror movies. The only problem is I get real scared. If I'm with a girl, I'm more scared than the girl."

Besides taking his special someone to the movies, Danny confides that the perfect way to spend an evening is to just get to know each other. "We could be anywhere," he says. "As long as we are spending time together, talking and learning about each other, that's what really counts."

MEET JORDAN KNIGHT

Jordan feels the same way as Danny about getting to know a girl. He likes wearing clothes he describes as "hip street stuff." Serious-minded and a perfectionist, Jordan is a thinker. His favorite play is *Julius Caesar*. Sometimes he is shy when he first meets people. He hasn't dated anyone steady yet, but this New Kid has a pretty good idea of the kind of girl who turns his head.

"I like petite girls who are charming, like to have fun, are loving, and have a great sense of humor," says Jordan. He thinks a great date would be on a secluded beach at night with a fire.

Jordan sports a unique hairstyle. He has a side part and a long braid. He's learning how to play the guitar and already plays keyboards. No matter how hard he tries, Jordan can't shake the habit of biting his nails. His Siamese cats are named Buster and Misty.

MEET JON KNIGHT

To Jordan's brother Jon, communication is important in a relationship. In the past, this handsome and confident talent has described his dream girl as "someone who is easy to talk to and is fun to be with." His idea of the perfect date is "doing anything, being anywhere as long as you're with the one you love."

Jon just may have found the right girl— he recently began dating Tiffany. Though they've often denied rumors that they're dating, on their last tour together, Tiffany and Jon discovered that they had many things in common and began spending a great deal of time together.

The only problem with this is that the New Kids and Tiffany are now on separate tours. The question is, how can these two superstar singers keep their long-distance relationship going? Of course, it is rough, but there is always a way. The two communicate with each other by talking on the phone.

Jon is nicknamed GQ, after the men's fashion magazine, because he loves shopping for clothes. Music, however, is what he loves most, and he enjoys playing the trumpet. Jon admires all the dance steps of the old Motown groups and describes his own dancing style as "like the old stuff, but I like to step with a little more energy."

★

MEET JOE McINTYRE

Last, but certainly not least, is Joe McIntyre, the kid who is referred to as "the major heartthrob of the group." The only New Kid with blue eyes, Joe describes himself as "funny, somewhat of a wise guy, worried, and chilled."

Joe prefers hanging out in comfortable clothes, and although he's determined to be a musical success, his most important goal is to have peace of mind. Joe, who describes himself as "funny and peaceful," is very concerned with problems in the world, such as war, poverty, and drugs. He claims that if he had one wish he'd would like to end homelessness.

Charming, friendly, and caring, Joe says his favorite kind of girls are "nice, cool, smart, chilled, and fine. She also has to have a fabulous sense of humor."

And what is Joe's idea of a great date? "I like doing the traditional things on a date like going to the movies or to a restaurant," he says. "But the ultimate place to spend time with a girl is going to Disney World. With all the rides and exhibits, you can't miss having a great time!"

★ ★ ★

While all five guys are looking forward to settling down with the girl of their dreams someday, they are in no rush. They know they have plenty of time to think about serious relationships. Right now, they are enjoying their roles as single heartthrobs and America's newest teen idols!

8

LIFE ON THE ROAD

What is it like being a top rock star living on the road? For each of the New Kids, it's a lot of hard work. It's often stressful and there's not much time for rest, but they're quick to tell people that it's fun.

It's plain to see that these guys have remained levelheaded and unspoiled by success. The truth is, they don't feel like celebrities and haven't yet adjusted to being treated like stars. But even though success hasn't changed the New Kids themselves, their lifestyles have certainly changed since they hit it big.

While the New Kids are enjoying life at the top, they are still trying to get used to the lack of privacy that comes with being public figures. The more popular they became, the more they found themselves being mobbed by groups of female admirers.

The first sign of their leap into stardom occurred during a concert they did with Tiffany in Cincinnati, Ohio. At the time, they were still unaware of the kind of success they were about to achieve, so they were really amazed that people were recognizing them backstage. Sure, they were used to being stopped and asked to sign autographs, but that was nothing compared to what happened at that concert. That night, Jordan and Donnie experienced one of their first encounters with overzealous fans.

"We tried to get backstage before Tiffany was finished with her show, so we wouldn't get caught up in the crowd," said Donnie, grinning. "But we didn't get there in time and ended up being attacked by about a thousand girls!

"The funny thing was that Jon was already backstage, Joe wasn't recognized because he had a hood over his head, and Danny wasn't recognized either because he wears his glasses offstage and he also had on a beach hat. So Jordan and I were the ones who got trapped by all those girls!"

Jon has an even better fan story that he loves to tell. "I was at a hotel and I was sitting in the Jacuzzi by the pool," he says. "Suddenly, all these girls came running into the hotel and ran toward me. They all stood around me and watched me in the Jacuzzi. I felt like a fish in an aquarium."

Even though it sometimes gets tough being swarmed by fans and having to sign autographs, the New Kids always try their best to keep their fans satisfied. "Our managers tell us not to talk to our fans when we're staying at hotels because it disrupts the other guests," concedes Jordan. "But we can't help it. We appreciate them following our careers and supporting us and we want them to know we care."

The guys will often go out of their way to meet their loyal admirers, even though there are times when their schedule just does not allow it. "It breaks our hearts if we have to tell someone we can't stop and sign autographs," offers Jon. "But sometimes we have to catch a plane or get to a rehearsal and our security guards have to pull us away!"

The New Kids make up for these times by answering as much of their fan mail as they can. Jordan, who admits that he doesn't have time to write to his family while on tour, will take the time to send out autographed photos to people who write to him.

In fact, for Valentine's Day in 1989, Jordan sent out over two hundred Valentine greetings to fans all over the United States, Japan, and Europe!

It is no secret that fame has a high price, but the New Kids aren't complaining. They say they are more than willing to pay it—even if it means spending more time on the road than at home. In the past few years, the New Kids have traveled from the smallest towns to the biggest cities in the United States and to faraway places like Japan, Hawaii, and European capitals.

There are advantages and disadvantages to doing so much traveling. Jon says, "We've made new friends in every city we've traveled to and I think that's great." Yet, although meeting new people and seeing different places is interesting and fun, there are times when the New Kids miss being home with their families.

"Sometimes I have to tell myself not to think of home," says Joe, who takes his teddy bear with him to fend off the feeling of homesickness. "I have to put everything aside and just work."

Since they've been going on tour, the guys have a new way of keeping in touch with their families. They each wear a beeper on their belt when they are on the road so they can be easily contacted by their parents at any time. When one of their beepers sounds, it means to call home and check in with the family. It helps the guys feel at ease when being so far from home. "If there's an emergency, it's easier for our folks to let us know," says Joe. "We talk to them all the time."

The New Kids travel in a tour bus to get from one city to the next, and Donnie admits, "It does get hectic living on the road. You snap at the other guys, and it's tough sleeping on the bus."

They try to make their grueling schedule fun by taking all the comforts of home with them. Since they now have three buses to carry the backup band, bodyguards, equipment, and crew, the New Kids have one bus to themselves—and it is complete with everything they need. There are five beds where the guys rest between shows; in the rear of the bus is an area Jon calls "the living room," with a refrigerator, stereo, sofa, TV, a VCR, and a selection of Nintendo video games and movies (including some of the guys' favorites, such as *Tootsie*, *Fright Night*, *Rambo*, and *St. Elmo's Fire*).

After every show, the New Kids usually have a ten-to-twelve-hour drive to the next concert date. In between sleeping, Jordan, who brings his small keyboards with him, usually finds time alone to work on a song, while the other guys play video games.

There are also times when fellow musicians will join the guys on the bus. When Sweet Sensation members Betty Le Bron, Margie Fernandez, and Sheila Vega opened for the New Kids, they spent time in between shows watching videos and playing games with them.

Other times, all five New Kids will just sit in a circle and talk. "We've been talking a lot about our favorite toys when we were younger," says Jon. "Things like Hot Wheels cars. We all agree they were our favorite childhood toys."

Do the New Kids *really* get along? Like all close friends, the New Kids admit that they occasionally have a disagreement. "We fight, but we get over it pretty fast," says Jordan. It's true that these five music-makers don't usually stay mad for very long. Although Joe doesn't forgive and forget so fast. Jon says, "The thing about Joe is that he holds a grudge longer than the rest of us." But in no time, the guys are usually back to clowning around and playing practical jokes on each other.

Since being on the road has become such a big part of their lives, Jordan exclaims that he sometimes doesn't even know what city or state the New Kids' bus has stopped in. "I woke up one day and said, 'Where are we?' " said this cute guy, smiling.

As the oldest New Kid, it is Jon, along with their road manager, Peter Work, who always makes sure everything is running on schedule. Jon is a very organized guy who likes keeping things neat, so it isn't surprising to see him picking up after the other guys. For instance, when they pull their tour bus into a new city for the night, Jon will often clean up the bus before it hits the road again. He also takes it upon himself to make sure all the laundry is washed and folded before the kids move on. "We've been doing our wash at home for a long time now, so we're used to it," he says.

In between traveling to their concert engagements, the guys have appeared on TV shows such as *Arsenio Hall* and *Dance Party U.S.A.*, as well as filming videos and attending awards shows.

The New Kids' hometown triumph came at the Boston Music Awards on April 25, 1989, when their song "(You Got It) The Right Stuff" was named Outstanding R&B Single and Outstanding Music Video.

"Forget Bobby Brown," raved the *Boston Herald.* "Forget Tracey Chapman. Tuesday night's ceremony for the third annual Boston Music Awards belonged to five teens from Dorchester—New Kids on the Block, who put on a performance before the hometown fans that literally shook the Wang Center. They sang, danced, and strutted . . . and kept the young female fans, who made up the majority of the crowd, screaming with delight."

The New Kids have often commented that they don't have as much free time as they did before success came their way, but they admit they are having twice as much fun.

What do the guys do when they come home after a long tour? "The thing I look forward to most is coming home and sleeping in my own bed," says Joe, and the rest of the band agrees.

When they have some time to rest, the guys chill out by doing mellow things like going to a movie or playing basketball, but their time off the road doesn't last too long. "Usually, we get home for about two days. And then our manager calls us and says, 'You boys have to start working again,'" says Joe, but he adds with a smile, "I never mind not being able to relax with my friends at home, because I can still chill out with Donnie, Danny, Jordan, and Jon on the road. We're like brothers!"

9

TEEN ROLE MODELS

"I think it's nice that so many kids are looking up to us," says a serious Jon Knight. "I want the group to be a role model to young people."

As the band's popularity soared, the New Kids felt it necessary to speak out to other kids. They immediately became involved in the Just Say No to Drugs campaign, and they've worked endless hours for the organization. They are hoping kids take their advice and stay off drugs.

This issue is important to them because Donnie claims all the guys felt pressure to take drugs when they were in school. Though none of the New Kids would ever get involved in any kind of substance abuse, one of Donnie's brothers was sent to prison because of drugs. For him it's a subject that really hits home.

"We're not only educated in books," Donnie reasons. "We're educated in life."

It was that real-life education they wanted to pass on to the youth of America. Speaking out to groups of high school students about the dangers of drugs, the New Kids became further involved in a cause they completely believed in.

Monday, March 13, 1989, was an important day for the New Kids. In the morning, they appeared at a high school in Massapequa, Long Island, where they talked to students about saying no to drugs. They performed a few of their songs, then got right down to business, telling kids to stay in school and stay out of trouble.

In an interview that afternoon, Donnie said, "We feel it's important to reach out to school kids because they're our fans and our peers."

After their appearance, the guys were whisked away and flown by helicopter to the WWOR-TV studios in Secaucus, New Jersey, where they appeared on the Sunday-morning show *Steampipe Alley*, performing for a studio audience of twenty-five students from a Hackensack, New Jersey, school.

The New Kids also joined Massachusetts

governor Michael Dukakis's statewide campaign against drugs, performing at various antidrug rallies, including the Governor's Alliance Against Drugs. They recorded a rap song with Boston mayor Raymond L. Flynn, which, Jon says, "told kids to just be yourself and don't be doing drugs."

On Monday, April 24, 1989, the New Kids were honored for their work with the antidrug campaign when Governor Dukakis declared the day "New Kids on the Block Day." Mindy Lubber, a spokeswoman for Dukakis, told *Newsweek,* "The group has played a very important role in the community's saying no to drugs. They've taken their popularity and used it as a platform."

Another important charity the guys give their time to is United Cerebral Palsy. In January 1989, they appeared for the third consecutive year on the nationally televised United Cerebral Palsy Telethon. They have done so much for this cause that the UCP named the band national teen spokesmen.

On April 30, 1989, the kids once again gave their support when they participated in the 16th Annual Bike-A-Thon for UCP in New York City. It took place in the heart of Manhattan's Central Park where over 3,000 bicycle riders raised more than $750,000 for UCP.

The photogenic New Kids had a blast that day, making sure everyone was satisfied. Besides taking part in the biking, the kids posed for countless photographs all over Central Park and met and talked with everyone who attended. Those who attended could see after meeting the New Kids on that sunny spring day that they were terrific and caring people.

As their involvement with worthy causes demonstrates, there is so much more to these five supertalented guys than most people really know. First of all, they feel very closely tied to their families. When they went to Hawaii for Christmas, 1988, they all treated their moms to a vacation. Only Joe's mom couldn't go because she doesn't like to fly in planes. But to make up for her missing out on a perfect vacation, Joe says, "I bought her a fur coat. When I called her from Hawaii, she said, 'Joseph, I'm walking around in my fur coat.'"

Donnie's mom, who is divorced from his dad, has attended all of the New Kids' shows and is very proud of her son. When Donnie is asked whom he admires the most, he is quick to answer, "My mom, because when I'm away from her, I realize what a good person she is. How strong a person she really is, how she spent all her life trying to make people happy. And she's done a great job of doing it, too."

For a while, Donnie resented his parents' decision to get divorced and his mother's remarrying. It was a difficult change in his life, but he learned to accept it. He's often talked to the Knight brothers, whose parents are also divorced, about the adjustments and changes divorce brings to a family's lifestyle.

Even though Donnie comes from a family of nine children, he says, "We all went our separate ways. My younger brother and me are with my mom, two of my brothers stayed with my dad, and everyone else is on their own."

To their fans, the guys seem bubbly and outgoing, and it doesn't seem like anything bothers them. Yet, when Danny revealed in an interview how he was dealing with recent deaths in his family, his fans got a chance to see a completely different side of this sensitive guy.

Since 1986, Danny's uncle, aunt, cousin, and grandfather have all passed away, and he says, "I've had a hard time dealing with it. It takes a lot of time to get over, but I know I will in time. I still think about them."

Like all young people, the New Kids have

experienced growing pains. They've had their share of trying times, some sad times, but also many happy times. They are well-adjusted young men who feel fortunate to be in a position to be role models and offer advice to other kids. They are proud to be in the league with other top teen singers who are also setting a good example for kids.

Donnie explains, "I'm proud of the groups that are out there because they are all so positive. New Edition, Tiffany, Debbie Gibson, and New Kids on the Block are all trying to be role models to today's kids. I just hope what we're doing helps because kids are the future."

10

INTO THE FUTURE

Often, when a band reaches dizzying heights of success in a relatively short period of time, rumors circulate that one member of the group is planning to leave. The New Kids have not been exempt from rumors. While they were in the middle of their sold-out tour, a story leaked into magazines about the exit of a band member.

Was this true? And if so, which New Kid was going to leave? A spokesperson for the band immediately made a statement to the press that the rumor was not true and that none of the five members had any intentions of leaving just yet.

Though the rumor continued to spread, the New Kids had their own discussions about the future and what it would hold for them.

The guys know that the next few years are crucial in maintaining their incredible popularity. They are ready for whatever happens in the years ahead because they believe in themselves and the message they are conveying to their audiences.

Though some people feel the New Kids are just another manufactured teen band, the members feel they are much more. "I trust that the public sees us as five individuals working together as a unit," says Donnie. "New Kids on the Block is a serious role. There is no puppeteer or someone else who is running things, having us do what they want us to do like with a lot of other young groups. We make most of the decisions for ourselves. We are five very creative guys doing things our own way."

No one knows for sure what made the New Kids finally click with audiences and become stars. It could've been when their third consecutive top-ten pop single, "I'll Be Loving You (Forever)," bulleted up *Billboard*'s charts. It could've been when *Billboard*'s Paul Grein declared them the first teen vocal group in history to score three top-three hits off one album. Their popularity with fans could've happened when they swept the Boston Music Awards, or maybe because their music has been so successful on all the music charts, including pop, R&B, and soul.

One thing that is certain is that the dream of superstardom came true for the New Kids. They found their audience and it is a huge and loving one. The public has made it known that they like what the New Kids have to say, and fans eagerly await a new collection of their fun, hip music.

For the New Kids, it seems every new step they take is a major breakthrough. When they appeared on Walt Disney World's July 4th Special, word spread that Disney executives were so impressed by the five young singers that they approached them to star in their very own movie.

This exciting new venture will, undoubtedly, secure the New Kids' name in show business as they branch out into another aspect of the entertainment business. They haven't publicly discussed the project, but it will be done sometime soon.

Jordan has commented about the band's preparation for their debut film by saying, "Everything that's been happening to us, we keep writing down. If something funny happens, we say 'Remember that for the movie' and put it on tape, just so we have some ideas for the movie."

In addition to the New Kids' theatrical film debut, plans are also under way for a New Kids Saturday-morning cartoon in the tradition of the half-hour Beatles cartoons in the 1960s and the Jackson 5 and Osmonds cartoons in the 1970s.

New Kids fans want as much as they can get on their five favorite guys, and over the past few months, stores have been bombarded with New Kids merchandise, from posters to T-shirts to a video of the group performing their famous songs.

There's more New Kids stuff still on the way. The band is so popular that when Columbia Records rereleased their debut album, it was met with an enormous demand. Before it even hit stores, the advance orders sold out and had to be reordered.

Whatever else the New Kids plan to do in the years to come, they will continue to make music and release records. They have now joined that select circle of artists whose albums are certified million-sellers even before the public has heard them.

It is certain, though, that the New Kids will continue to change and grow musically, to mature and learn. "We are growing up," says Donnie. "I don't think when we are twenty-five years old, we will be singing about the same things we are singing about now. It is just nature. I don't think it is anything that we have to brag about, growing with our music. It's just the nature of people."

The New Kids are working at an unprecedented speed, recording and churning out more music than ever before. One very special project is their Christmas album, which was released this past September. Titled *New Kids on the Block—Merry, Merry Christmas*, it contains ten songs, including favorite Christmas standards such as "White Christmas," "The Christmas Song," and "Little Drummer Boy" and six hot new tracks all written by Maurice Starr. Donnie cowrote *Funky, Funky Xmas*, a fun rap song, with Starr; and both Donnie and Danny coproduced the song with Starr.

Because Christmas is such a special holiday to the New Kids, they worked long hours recording the album. It begins and ends with "This One's for the Children" with lead vocals by Jordan and Donnie and backgrounds by New Kids with the Morning Star Baptist Church Choir and the Voices of Innocence of the Charles Street A.M.E. Church. The album is appropriately dedicated to the children of the world.

In addition to recording a limited edition Christmas album, the New Kids went back into the studio and laid down tracks for their follow-up to *Hangin' Tough*. Donnie says, "I think the whole band agrees that our next album is going to be better than *Hangin' Tough*. It's definitely a step up for the New Kids. Jordan, Danny, and me wrote four songs and we're producing two songs."

Professionally, all five New Kids would like to see the band enjoy years of success. Personally, the guys each have their own separate dreams and aspirations. Donnie, thinking ahead five or ten years down the road, says, "I'd like to have a family. A small family and a house."

Danny would like to become a recording engineer and help other kids break into the business. Jordan states realistically, "I plan on becoming a record producer, songwriter, and maybe even a solo artist. Who knows what will happen in the future. I know there will be a day when I won't be part of this band anymore. You know the old saying 'All good things must come to an end.' I know the group won't last forever. But before that happens, I want to be sure I give as much as I can to the New Kids."

At this stage in their careers the New Kids look back on everything that has happened to them with awe, wonder, and happiness. After five years of playing in small theaters, clubs, and amusement parks, they are now selling out in arenas—The Meadowlands Stadium in New Jersey, Nassau Coliseum in Long Island, and Madison Square Garden in New York. Still, the New Kids aren't completely satisfied.

"This is only the beginning," states Donnie with determination. "We want to go back out and do more. Whatever we did before we want to double. If people thought we were great then, the next time we go out we want to be even better."

The New Kids on the Block are ready to accomplish more than they already have. They want to grow as performers, songwriters, and maybe even actors.

New Kids on the Block have moved in. And it shouldn't be any surprise to anyone if they decide to stay in the neighborhood for a long time to come.

DISCOGRAPHY

New Kids on the Block
 (Columbia, 1986; rereleased, 1989)

    Stop It Girl
    Didn't I (Blow Your Mind)
    Popsicle
    Angel
    Be My Girl
    New Kids on the Block
    Are You Down?
    I Wanna Be Loved by You
    Don't Give Up on Me
    Treat Me Right

New Kids on the Block—Hangin' Tough
 (Columbia, 1988)

    (You Got It) The Right Stuff
    Please Don't Go Girl
    I'll Be Loving You (Forever)
    Cover Girl
    I Need You
    Hangin' Tough

I Remember When
What'cha Gonna Do (About It)
My Favorite Girl
Hold On

New Kids on the Block—
Merry, Merry Christmas
   (Columbia, 1989)

   This One's for the Children
   Last Night I Saw Santa Claus
   I'll Be Missin' You Come Christmas (A
      Letter to Santa)
   I Still Believe in Santa Claus
   Merry, Merry Christmas
   The Christmas Song (Chestnuts
      Roasting on an Open Fire)
   Funky, Funky Xmas
   White Christmas
   Little Drummer Boy
   This One's for the Children (Reprise)

VIDEOGRAPHY

MUSIC VIDEOS

Please Don't Go Girl
You Got It (The Right Stuff)
I'll Be Loving You (Forever)
Hangin' Tough

VIDEO CASSETTE

New Kids on the Block—Hangin' Tough
(CBS Home Video, 1989)

Contains a behind-the-scenes, candid glimpse of the personalities and antics of the New Kids . . . offstage and on the road. Plus, their four smash videos from their multiplatinum album, *Hangin' Tough.*

1. Please Don't Go Girl
2. You Got It (The Right Stuff)
3. I'll Be Loving You (Forever)
4. Hangin' Tough

Running time: 30 minutes

NEW KIDS
VITAL STATISTICS

JORDAN KNIGHT

Full real name: Jordan Nathaniel Marcel Knight
Nickname: "J"
Birthdate: May 17, 1971
Birthplace: Worcester, Massachusetts
Eye color: Dark brown
Hair color: Brown
Height: 5'10"
Weight: 155 lbs.
Parents: Marlene Putnam and Allan Knight
Brothers & sisters: Allison, Sharon, David, Chris, fellow New Kid Jon
Pets: Siamese cats, Buster and Misty
Current residence: Boston, Massachusetts

Hobbies: Basketball, going to clubs, reading magazines

First job: Camp counselor

Favorite foods: Lasagna, Italian, Chinese

Favorite drink: Chocolate milk shake

Favorite actor: Robert DeNiro

Favorite TV shows: *The Cosby Show, America's Most Wanted*

Favorite movies: *Soul Man, Robocop, The Untouchables*

Favorite place: "Boston, Massachusetts, because I grew up there and I still live there. Also the South because it's warm and beautiful."

Favorite pastime: Going to the beach

Favorite kind of girl: "I like a loving girl. One who likes to have fun and show her feelings."

Favorite date: "On a secluded beach at night with a fire."

Favorite book: *Jonathan Livingston Seagull*

Favorite sport: Basketball

Favorite song: "You Make Me Feel Brand-New" by The Stylistics

Favorite childhood memory: "Singing in the church choir."

Scariest childhood experience: "Being chased by a man with a gun who thought I was writing on his store."

Instrument played: Keyboards

Biggest thrill: Hearing a New Kids song on the radio for the first time

Biggest disappointment: Having that same song flop

Biggest fear: The supernatural

Biggest influence on his life: "My mother and my producer because they taught me to shoot for the best."

Best quality: "I don't worry too much."

Worst quality: "I don't let myself sleep enough."

Most memorable experience with New Kids: "Playing at the Apollo Theater in New York."

Habits: "I bite my nails and put ketchup on everything. I also twirl and pull my hair."

What makes Jordan happy: "Seeing all my hard work pay off."

What makes Jordan sad: "Leaving home to go on tour."

Message to fans: "Keep faith in the New Kids and we will always be there for you."

Where to write to Jordan:
Jordan Knight
c/o New Kids on the Block
P.O. Box 7080
Quincy, MA 02269

JON KNIGHT

Full real name: Jonathan Rashleigh Knight

Nickname: "GQ"

Birthdate: November 29, 1968

Birthplace: Worcester, Massachusetts

Eye color: Hazel

Hair color: Brown

Height: 5'11"

Weight: 155 lbs.

Parents: Marlene Putnam and Allan Knight

Brothers & sisters: Allison, Sharon, David, Chris, fellow New Kid Jordan

First record bought: "I don't know. Probably 'Mickey Mouse Sings,'" he says with a smile.

Favorite childhood memory: "Spending summers at my grandparents' cottage in Canada."

Favorite city: "Boston, because it's home and home is the best place to be."

Favorite holiday: Easter

Favorite sports: Skiing, swimming

Favorite colors: Black and white

Favorite TV shows: *The Cosby Show, Thirtysomething*

Favorite food: Italian

Favorite fast food: Burger King

Favorite junk foods: Chocolate and Hostess cupcakes

Favorite drinks: Chocolate and strawberry milk shakes

Favorite music: R&B and pop. "I hate heavy metal," he says.

Biggest influence on his life: "My mom, because she taught me to be a good person."

Pet peeve: "I hate eggs!"

Shoe size: 10½

Shirt size: Large

Main goal: To be the best at everything he does

Most memorable moment: "Hearing a New Kids song on the radio for the first time."

What makes Jon happy: Peace on earth

What makes Jon sad: War and indifference

Ideal girl: "Sweet, smart, independent, and honest. Someone I can talk to and is fun to be with."

Best quality: "My good nature toward things and people."

Worst quality: "Nothing. I'm very confident with myself, but not conceited."

People Jon admires: "Everyone involved with making the New Kids number one, especially our producer, Maurice Starr."

Message to fans: "Love yourself and others so we can make our world a better place."

Where to write to Jon:

Jon Knight
c/o New Kids on the Block
P.O. Box 7080
Quincy, MA 02269

JOE McINTYRE

Full real name: Joseph Mulrey McIntyre
Nicknames: Joe Bird, Joey Joe
Birthdate: December 31, 1972
Birthplace: Needham, Massachusetts
Eye color: Blue
Hair color: Blondish brown
Height: 5'6"
Weight: 120 lbs.
Parents: Thomas and Kay
Brothers & sisters: Judith, Alice, Susan, Patricia, Carol, Jean, Kate, Tom
Current residence: Boston, Massachusetts
Favorite food: Mexican
Favorite drink: Classic Coke, anything nonalcoholic
Favorite clothes: "Anything comfortable!"
Favorite colors: Blue, red
Favorite bands: Huey Lewis and the News, The Temptations
Favorite movies: *Big, Beverly Hills Cop, Midnight Run*
Favorite TV show: *Cheers*

Favorite childhood memory: "Christmas days with my family and taking a walk with my sister in the snow."

Favorite actors: Bill Cosby, Robert DeNiro

Favorite actress: His sister Judith

Favorite cars: Jaguar, BMW with phone

Astrological sign: Capricorn

Biggest influence on his life: His family and friends

Musical instrument played: He's studying the piano.

Traveling companion: His teddy bear

Shoe size: 8½

Shirt size: Small

Hobbies: Basketball, bowling

Main goals: "To be rich and famous, but most of all, to have peace of mind."

Ideal girl: "Cool, chill, smart, and fine."

What makes Joe happy: Peace

What makes Joe sad: War

Self-description: "Funny and peaceful."

Where to write to Joe:

Joe McIntyre
c/o New Kids on the Block
P.O. Box 7080
Quincy, MA 02269

DONNIE WAHLBERG

Full real name: Donald E. Wahlberg, Jr.
Nicknames: Donnie, Dennis Cheese
Birthdate: August 17, 1969
Birthplace: Dorchester, Massachusetts
Eye color: Hazel
Hair color: Blondish brown
Height: 5'10"
Weight: 155 lbs.
Parents: Donald, Sr., and Alma
Brothers & sisters: Michelle, Debbie, Paul, Arthur, Jimbo, Tracey, Bob, Mark
Current residence: Dorchester, Massachusetts
Instrument played: Drums
Favorite food: "My dad's home cooking!"
Favorite drinks: Water, apple juice, Coca-Cola
Favorite breakfast cereal: Count Chocula
Favorite holiday: "My birthday!"
Favorite cartoon character: Dennis the Menace
Favorite colors: Black and gold
Favorite book: *Old Yeller*

Favorite sports: Baseball, basketball
Favorite singer: Bobby Brown
Favorite movie: *Scarface*
Favorite song: "Please Don't Go Girl"
Favorite car: Saab 900 convertible
Favorite music: Dance music
Favorite TV show: *Sesame Street*
Favorite actress: Cher
Favorite actor: Al Pacino
Favorite vacation spots: Hawaii and Alaska
Shoe size: 8
Shirt size: Large
Best qualities: "I'm kind, giving, and tons of fun."
Most memorable moment: "Getting a standing ovation at New York's Apollo Theater."
Worst quality: "I'm very impatient!"
Worst habit: Eating too much junk food
Hobbies: Drawing, dancing
Ideal girl: "Someone with a strong personality who likes to have fun and is very independent."
Ideal date: "Dinner at a quiet restaurant, movie, and a walk around Boston."
Self-description: "I'm very generous, very serious. I love talking and I'm always thinking. I love to be in love."

Main goal: "To succeed, but have fun doing it."

Message to fans: "Peace out! Say no to drugs!"

Where to write to Donnie:

Donnie Wahlberg
c/o New Kids on the Block
P.O. Box 7080
Quincy, MA 02269

DANNY WOOD

Full real name: Daniel William Wood, Jr.

Nicknames: Puff McCloud, Woody the Woodpecker

Birthdate: May 14, 1970

Birthplace: Boston, Massachusetts

Eye color: Brown

Hair color: Black

Height: 5'8"

Weight: 145 lbs.

Parents: Daniel, Sr., and Elizabeth

Brothers & sisters: Bethany, Pam, Brett, Rachel, Melissa

Current residence: Boston, Massachusetts

Favorite sport: Basketball

Favorite musician: Maurice Starr

Favorite book: *The Autobiography of Malcolm X*

Favorite band: One Nation

Favorite movies: *The Terminator, Stand By Me, Star Wars*

Favorite actor: Kevin Costner

Favorite actress: Cher

Favorite TV show: *The Cosby Show*

Favorite car: Cherokee Jeep

Favorite foods: Roast beef, Chinese, Italian, chicken

Favorite snack: Fruit

Favorite drink: Water

Favorite vacation spot: Florida

Favorite song: "Some Things Never Change" by The Stylistics

Favorite cartoon character: Woody Woodpecker

Favorite holiday: Christmas

Favorite childhood memory: "When my little sister Rachel was born."

Scariest childhood memory: Falling off his bicycle

First record bought: "Let's Dance" by David Bowie

Hobby: Playing basketball

Ideal girl: "Nice, cute, funny, easygoing."

Ideal date: "Just spending time with a special girl getting to know each other."

Pastime: Writing songs

Shoe size: 8½

Shirt size: Medium

Self-description: "Stubborn, easygoing, determined."

Best quality: "Hardworking. I don't crack under pressure."

Main goal: To be successful

First ambition: To be an architect

Worst habit: Getting defensive

Biggest like: Performing onstage

Biggest dislike: Prejudice

Most prized moments: "The time I spend with my mom!"

Future plans: "To have fun, go to the top, see lots of platinum albums, and be a top recording engineer."

Message to fans: "Stay off the streets and hold on to your dreams."

Where to write to Danny:

Danny Wood
c/o New Kids on the Block
P.O. Box 7080
Quincy, MA 02269

NEW KIDS QUOTES

On Performing Onstage

"I love doing the shows. I love being onstage with my friends."

—*Danny*

"The last few shows we've done, there's been a lot of people coming toward us and throwing gifts onto the stage. Sometimes it can be scary."

—*Jon*

"It's shocking at first. One night we did a show and when we came out on stage, the place was packed. All we could see were these lights flashing."

—*Joe*

★

"You don't ever know what's going to happen during any show. But any new challenge is good. I just love to be with the crowd!"

—*Donnie*

On Fans

"We're not these big, perfect, awesome dudes who can do anything, and I hope fans don't think we are. We're equal to our fans—in fact, we're just like them!"

—*Joe*

"Just because I can't meet as many fans as I'd like to doesn't mean that I can't relate to them. When I'm onstage, I use that time to let them know I care. Sometimes I'll point at someone or look straight into a fan's eyes just to let them know I'm there for them."

—*Jon*

On the Band's Debut Album

"I like to listen to our first album. But it was then, it's not for now. *Hangin' Tough* is what we like to listen to now."

—*Danny*

"When our first album didn't take off, we could've just given up. We could have forgotten the whole thing and stopped recording, but what kept us together was that we're such good friends."

—*Jordan*

On Changing the World

"I would change the way we treat the environment, like pollution."

—*Joe*

"I would like to meet Mikhail Gorbachev [the leader of the Soviet Union]. I think it would be great to sit in a room with him and talk about the situation in the world and try to make peace."

—*Donnie*

"It all goes back to the individual. People have to change themselves first before they can change the world. It's good to change yourself for the better, then the world will be a lot better. I wish that would happen. I'm hoping it's not too far away."

—*Danny*

On the Band

"We've got a lot of energy and excitement. I think that's why kids can relate to us."

—*Jordan*

"I really enjoy being in the group. Sure, rehearsals can be boring and there's a lot of hard work, but it's fun."

—*Jordan*

"A lot of people say we're all-American and clean-cut, and that's what we are. But we're all-city, too."

—*Danny*

"Everyone in the band is full of surprises, but I'm known as the most hyper one. I probably got that tag because I was out front at first at all our shows. I would be the lead, so I had to have more energy."

—*Donnie*

On Tiffany

"She's great. She's one of the nicest people you would want to meet. She's just genuinely nice. We all really like Tiffany a lot."

—*Donnie*

"We were very nervous when we first met Tiffany. We wanted to make a good impression because she's really talented. We literally tried out for her right in her dressing room. She felt so uneasy—these five kids that she had never met before auditioning to get on her tour. It was crazy! She felt out of place and we felt out of place. But she was really sweet and had a lot of consideration for us. She let us have a lot of things that opening acts don't usually have. But I think she felt that she was once in our place and she wanted to help us out."

—*Joe*

On Success

"When we go out onstage and the crowd reacts with screams and claps and waves, I feel like we've really succeeded at this. And that's a great feeling."

—*Danny*

"When we weren't famous, we were able to go out to clubs and hang out like normal people. Now, everybody stares—it can make us a little self-conscious."

—*Jordan*

About the Author

Grace Catalano is the author of the popular Bantam Starfire books *Kirk Cameron: Dream Guy*, *River Phoenix: Hero & Heartthrob*, and *Alyssa Milano: She's the Boss*. She has written *Teen Star Yearbook* and is currently the editor of three entertainment magazines, *Rock Legend* and the popular teen magazines *Dream Guys* and *Dream Guys Presents*. She also wrote *Elvis—A 10th Anniversary Tribute* and *Elvis and Priscilla*. Grace lives on the North Shore of Long Island.

All-Star Movie and TV Favorites
The Hottest Teen Heartthrobs!

These terrific star bios are packed with the juicy details *you* want to know. Here's the inside scoop on the star's family life, friends, tips on dating, life on the set, future career plans, *plus* fantastic photo inserts.

☐ ALYSSA MILANO: SHE'S THE BOSS by Grace Catalano   28158 $2.75

☐ RIVER PHOENIX: HERO AND HEARTTHROB by Grace Catalano   27728 $2.75

☐ KIRK CAMERON: DREAM GUY by Grace Catalano   27135 $2.75

Coming in February! Watch for
DEBBIE GIBSON: ELECTRIC STAR

☆ Plus...don't miss exciting movie and TV tie-ins of these top favorites!

☐ DEAD POETS SOCIETY by N.H. Kleinbaum   28298 $2.95

☐ HEAD OF THE CLASS by Susan Beth Pfeffer   28190 $2.95

Buy them at your local bookstore or use this handy coupon for ordering:

- -

Bantam Books, Dept. DA29, 414 East Golf Road, Des Plaines, IL 60016

Please send me the items I have checked above. I am enclosing $ ___
(please add $2.00 to cover postage and handling). Send check or .noney
order, no cash or C.O.D.s please.

Mr/Ms _____

Address _____

City/State _____ Zip _____

DA29–12/89

Please allow four to six weeks for delivery.
Prices and availability subject to change without notice.